The best job in the universe!

Astronaut

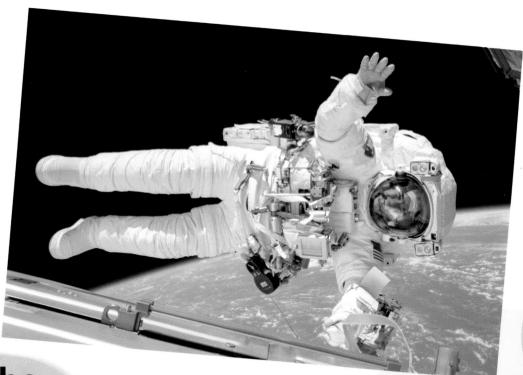

the
BIG
PICTURE

Angela Royston

Published 2010 by
A&C Black Publishers Ltd.
36 Soho Square, London, W1D 3QY

www.acblack.com

ISBN HB 978-1-4081-2785-8
PB 978-1-4081-3165-7

Text copyright © 2010 Angela Royston

This book is produced using paper that is made from wood grown in managed, sustainable forests. It is natural, renewable and recyclable. The logging and manufacturing processes conform to the environmental regulations of the country of origin.

Produced for A&C Black by Calcium. www.calciumcreative.co.uk

Printed and bound in China by C&C Offset Printing Co.

All the internet addresses given in this book were correct at the time of going to press. The author and publishers regret any inconvenience caused if addresses have changed or sites have ceased to exist, but can accept no responsibility for any such changes.

Acknowledgements

The publishers would like to thank the following for their kind permission to reproduce their photographs:

Cover: Shutterstock: Tischenko Irina (front), Alle (back). **Pages:** NASA: 4-5, 10-11, 20, Goddard Space Flight Center 6, Human Space Flight Collection 1, 9, 12-13, 14-15, 19, 21, 24, Johnson Space Center 3, 16-17, Marshall Space Flight Center 5; Shutterstock: Devation/Edwin Verbruggen 18-19, Dr_Flash 18, Eric G 8, Jean-Luc 14-15 (background), William Attard McCarthy 6-7 (background), Remy Bejear Merriex 8-9, Shukaylov Roman 20-21, Skobrik 10, Snaprender 2-3, 7, Ekaterina Starshaya 22-23, Taily 10-11 (background), 12-13 (background), Vicente Barcelo Varona 16-17 (background), WilleeCole 12

Contents

Blast Off!

A spacecraft **is on the launch pad. Inside are five** astronauts, **waiting to blast into** space.

Into the air

The **rockets** start up. Engines roar and the spacecraft lifts into the air.

5, 4, 3, 2, 1

Rocket power

A huge tank is filled with **fuel** for the spacecraft's engines. When the fuel is used up, the tank and **booster** rockets fall off, and back to Earth.

Two booster rockets help to power the spacecraft into the sky.

5

Into Space

Astronauts in space can see the Earth far below them. They can see blue oceans and white clouds.

Round and round

The spacecraft travels very fast. It **orbits** Earth. This means that it goes round and round Earth.

A spacecraft takes one and a half hours to orbit Earth.

Starlight

The spacecraft flies from light to dark as it orbits Earth. When it is dark, the astronauts see billions of bright stars.

Floating

The astronauts float inside the spacecraft. They push themselves off the walls to move about.

Stick it down!

Everything floats in space. Astronauts stick things to **Velcro** patches on the spacecraft walls to stop them floating away.

Watch out!

No gravity

On Earth, a **force** called gravity pulls you down to the ground. There is no gravity in space so everything floats!

Floating in space is easier than swimming in water

9

Dinner Time

The food astronauts eat is cooked on Earth before they leave. It is then packed into the spacecraft.

Drink up

Astronauts drink through straws from containers. If they used a cup, all the liquid would float away in tiny drops!

Snack attack

Floating food

Astronauts heat food in the spacecraft oven. They have to eat it very carefully – if they move the spoon too fast it will float away!

It's not easy to eat in space!

Bathtime

Astronauts have a special shower in the spacecraft. They cannot just turn on the tap to get water!

No splashes in space!

Astronauts wash with a damp sponge. They use special shampoo to wash their hair. It does not need to be rinsed out.

Scrub-a-dub!

Drying off

Astronauts use a machine like a small vacuum cleaner, which sucks all the water off their bodies.

We still use towels to dry our hair!

13

Hold on Tight

The astronauts' sleeping bags are fixed to the wall. This stops them floating while they are asleep!

Sleep well

Straps hold the astronaut onto the bed and help them to lie flat.

Zzzzzz

Astronauts still dream in space.

Toilets too!

An astronaut even has to strap himself to the toilet. Air sucks away everything in the toilet so it can't escape!

Spacewalk

Sometimes, astronauts have to work outside the spacecraft. Then they wear a spacesuit.

Staying alive

The spacesuit gives air and everything else the astronaut needs to stay alive.

Astronauts are tied to the spacecraft so they do not float away.

Helmet

Space danger

There is no air to breathe in space. Without a spacesuit, the astronaut would die. The spacesuit also stops the astronaut getting too hot or cold.

Gloves

Hello Earth!

The astronauts are alone in space, but they can talk to people back on Earth.

In control

From space, the astronauts talk to Mission Control. This is a group of people on Earth who control the space mission.

See you soon!

Hi there!

Astronauts can be in space for many months. They write **emails** to their families back on Earth. Sometimes, they can talk to their families by telephone.

Even in space, emails can be sent!

Back to Earth

To return to Earth, the astronauts slow the spacecraft down. Then it falls towards the Earth.

Time to land

As it nears the Earth, the spacecraft slows down and glides to the ground.

We're back!

Wobbly legs

It takes several days for the astronauts to get used to being back on Earth. Floating makes their muscles weak. They have to exercise to make them strong again.

The astronauts tell everyone about their space trip.

21

Glossary

astronauts people who travel into space

booster something that gives extra power

emails letters sent from one computer to another

force a push or a pull that changes the way something moves

fuel something that is burned to give heat or make an engine work

orbits travels in a path around something in space

rockets powerful engines that burn fuel very fast

space everything in the universe

spacecraft a vehicle that travels into space

spacesuit special clothes that allow an astronaut to survive in space outside the spacecraft

Velcro furry material that things can be stuck on to

Further Reading

Websites

Find out more about space at:
starchild.gsfc.nasa.gov/docs/StarChild/ space_level1/space.html

Learn about stars and planets at:
www.kidsastronomy.com

Find out more about space travel at:
www.space.com/spaceshuttle

Books

Astronauts (Graphic Careers) by David West, Franklin Watts (2010).

Astronauts Handbook by Meghan McCarthy, Alfred A. Knopf (2008).

Living in Space (Star Quest) by Angela Royston, Rigby (2005).

Index